ABC
GOD LOVES ME!

Gale Bradley

To order additional copies of this book, contact:
Xlibris Corporation
1-888-795-4274
www.Xlibris.com
Orders@Xlibris.com

God has a special love for me.

I am the apple of his eye.

Deuteronomy 32:10

♥ **Believe,**

Mark 9:23

he cares.

1 Peter 5:7

This is the day that the Lord has made.

Psalm 118:24

♥ I eat living bread.

John 6:35

♥ Set free.

John 8:32

In the morning I will praise
him, for the Lord is good.

Psalm 90:14

He is my hiding place.

Psalm 17:8

💜 **I'll praise him with my instruments.**

Ephesians 5:19

♥ **The joy of the Lord is my strength.**

Jeremiah 8:10

Greet me with a kiss.

Romans 16:16

♥ **Let's carry the load together.**

Galatians 6:2

15

♥ God's mercy endures forever.

1 Chronicles 16:34

He is near to each broken heart.

Psalm 34:18

♥ His banner over me is love.

Jeremiah 31:3

♥ **He keeps me in perfect peace.**

Isaiah 26:3

 19

♥ In faith, I can quench the feiry darts.

Ephesians 6:16

♥ He gives me rest.

Matthew 11:28

♥ **Be still, know that he is God.**

Psalm 46:10

<heart> **Taste and see that the Lord is good.**

Psalm 34:8

23

♥ **United we can do it.**

Psalm 133:1

♥ **He heard my voice.**

Psalm 6:9

❤ I drink the living water.

John 4:10

Joy   Salvation
Emmanuel   Beloved   Light
Strong Tower   Wonderful
Lamb of God   Word
Resting Place
Restorer
Prince of Peace   Mighty God
Hope
Glory Lovely

♥ **How excellent is his name.**

Psalm 8:1

❤ **His yoke is so easy.**

Matthew 11:30

💜 **There is a resting place in Zion.**

Psalm 48:2

♥ O how God loves me, with a
very special love.

I'd like to thank my mom for taking me to Sunday School and teaching me the ABC's of God's love.

A special acknowledgment to my pastor James Daniel and Sunday School Teachers everywhere!

Printed in the United States
by Baker & Taylor Publisher Services